Earthly Insights
from
The Council of 12

Earthly Insights from The Council of 12

by **KIJANA**

Copyright © 2022 by Kijana Martin

All rights reserved. This book or any portion thereof may not be reproduced or used in any manner whatsoever without the express written permission of the copyright owner.

Publisher: Kijana Martin
First Printing, 2022

DEDICATED TO
Every brave soul who has embraced and endured the Council of 12 teachings.

Contents

Introduction	a
The Simulation	1
Earth Is Not a Punishment	2
Fear Versus Love	3
All is Love	4
Balance	5
Existence	6
The Absence of Light	7
Acknowledge Existence	8
Connection	9
Higher Self	10
Gods	11
Energy	12
Perfection	13
Aspects	14
Perspective	15
Love Consciousness	16
Karma	17
Experience. Knowledge. Wisdom.	18
Gifts	19
Energy Transfer	20
Be	21
Spiritual Sight	22
Distractions	23
Everything is You	24
Earth	25
Reflections	26
Focus & Manifestation	27
Owning Your Story	28
Emotions Are Master Teachers	29
Triggers	30
Truth	31
Release Emotions	32
Forgiveness	33

Empty Words	34
Worry	35
Doubt	36
Moments	37
Energetic Signatures	38
Shhhh!	39
As Above, So Below	40
Healing	41
Kindness	42
The Ego	43
Limitations	44
Layers of Healing	45
Your Journey	46
Fear and Love Manifests	47
Belief vs Knowing	48
Raising Consciousness	49
Green	50
Illness	51
Discomfort	52
Love	53
Masculine Dominance	54
Feminine Imbalance	55
Feminine & Masculine Balance	56
Soul Ties	57
Twin Flames	58
Reflections of Love	59
Power of Observation	60
Authority	61
Fear and Desire	62
Nine Year Life Cycles	63
No One Owes You	64
Releasing Victimhood	65
Answers From Your Heart	66
Divination Tools	67
Your Voice	68
Fight or Ease	69

Health	70
That Is Not Love	71
To Flow	72
Failure is Not an Option	73
Stress	74
Letting Go	75
Blessings	76
Black. Dark. The Absence of Light.	77
Your Focus is Currency	78
Rejection	79
Boundaries	80
Tears, Laughter, and Screaming	81
The Root	82
Identity	83
Emotions + Words	84
Eliminate Dependency	85
Spirit Relationships	86
Your Frequency Shift	87
Unexpected Power	88
5D	89
Touch Soil	90
Gather and Share Knowledge	91
All That Is and Nothing	92
Sight and Sound	93
Happiness is a Distraction	94
Breaking Down	95
Harmony With Nature	96
Fright	97
Ghosts	98
Speak to Release	99
Languages Will Eventually Be Defunct	100
The Only Goal	101
About Kijana	103

Introduction

In 2016 I was introduced to the Council of 12 during a channel that was for me, through me. These master teachers took their time as they showed me their worlds, colors they favored, the animals they walk with, and gave me insights on every person that was important to me.

I was afraid and curious as I endured the channel and a massive headache for six hours. After it was over, I was afraid that I had been controlled by some beings and others had tried to as well.

Eventually, at a plant medicine gathering, I met a woman who helped me shield myself from predatory energies and I became a clear conduit for the Council of 12. That night, I channeled for ten hours providing individual guidance for over twenty people.

Since then, I have channeled the Council of 12 for hundreds of people. Their and my goal is to simplify this earthly experience and help you understand the power that you have in this reality.

I am here as a conduit, teacher, and guide, to help you remember who you are.

With love,
Kijana

The Simulation

The reality you live in is a simulation. There have been countless iterations of existence on this planet. You are experiencing one. Enjoy it.

Earth Is Not a Punishment

Returning to Earth is not a punishment. You requested to return to Earth to experience forgetting your power, who you are, and emotions. You are here to explore the path to love which begins with yourself.

Some beings would love to have this experience that you are having. Be appreciative that you are visiting a planet that is pure love in form.

Fear Versus Love

Fear, not hate, is the opposite of love. Emotions are born either from fear, like hate, or love, like joy.

The storyline of this reality is fear versus love. The question is, "Will the people of this reality realize they are being controlled by fear and that they, themselves are love?"

All is Love

Source is Love. Love is creation. All things are birthed from love. Like a cell in your body is an aspect of you, you are an aspect of Source experiencing itself.

Source is a body of energy and not the only one of its kind. There are many.

Balance

There is always a balance in creation. To understand a thing, you experience the opposite. Fear is the balance to love. Negative is the balance to positive.

Existence

Man will never know the vastness of existence. There is no end to creation. Creation is constantly doing what it was meant to do; create and expand.

The Absence of Light

Why are you afraid of the dark? You were created in darkness, or the absence of light, as all things are. The absence of light, as we like to call it, is the beginning of all things in existence. Everything in existence is within the absence of light.

Acknowledge Existence

Everything in existence wants to be acknowledged. Source had an amazing orgasm, known as the Big Bang. She created many aspects of herself, that keep creating, so she will never question whether she exists.

When something is acknowledged as existing, it is affirmed. When you acknowledge it, be it an element, a plant, or a friend, it wants to be of service.

Connection

Your connection to the spirit realm is within. By connecting to oneself, you connect to Source and everything in creation. This includes your ancestors, guides, master teachers, and your higher self.

Higher Self

Your higher self is essentially the energy you were birthed from. Your higher self houses all the experiences, of all the lives it has shared. It is the essence of you.

You tap into your essence when your mind and body rest. You honor your agreements in other realities, travel, and commune with other beings.

Gods

Man creates the gods he chooses to worship. Each god or deity was once a being that was believed to have walked the earth and done good deeds. Man recorded the story of that being and decided to worship them. They became a diety.

Man has lost sight that a god is a step above man. Man has the same abilities if he attunes to them.

Gods are masters of their craft and purpose. They are meant to partner and be of assistance to man during his earthly experience.

Gods, deities, or orishas require acknowledgment and offerings as energetic exchanges and acts of love. They can be called upon for assistance and released when they are not needed. You do not have to continually worship them.

Man has lost track of who he is; a spirit being, a cell of Source, having a human experience. You are not limited to being a god and playing a roll. You are Source, ALL that IS.

Energy

Everything is energy. Energy can never be destroyed. It can be transmuted or changed into something else.

When energy is acknowledged, it is eager to serve.

Your acknowledgment of energy reminds it of its existence, regardless of what it is.

Perfection

Everything in creation is perfectly created. There are no mistakes or errors, including what you call deformed. Remember, everyone and everything is you.

Every person or thing is perfect in design and purpose.

Aspects

There are many aspects of beings in creation as there are many aspects of self. Some beings lend their energy, an aspect of them, to you in this lifetime.

Beings can embody, complement, and/or guide you.

You may have been the being. You may have a relationship with the being. You may have an agreement for assistance in this lifetime.

Before claiming you are a particular being, clarify with that being for a deeper understanding.

Perspective

Do not trust the physical eyes as the only perspective for sight. What you see will not necessarily match what another sees. Perspectives change depending on experience and knowledge. There are layers to all realities and which layer you are witnessing will depend on your awareness.

The willingness to see things from a different perspective can alter your reality in a moment.

Love Consciousness

You have the power to change this reality's consciousness by changing yourself. Self-love raises the vibration and impacts the consciousness overall. By loving you, you teach others how to love themselves, through example.

Each one, teach one.

Karma

Karma is simply a lesson you have chosen for yourself in this lifetime because you may have experienced the opposite perspective in this or another lifetime. You are attempting to balance and completely understand a thing or experience.

Experience. Knowledge. Wisdom.

Experience begets knowledge and knowledge begets wisdom.

To know something, you will have experienced it, or proof has been demonstrated for it to be accepted as known.

When there is an experience that results in fact, what you know to be undeniably true in your experience, then you have wisdom.

Gifts

It is natural to feel other's energy. It is natural to dream prophetically. It is natural to heal with energy through your hands. It is natural to be telepathic and all the other things that you have been conditioned to believe to be abnormal or special.

Everyone chooses which gifts they will use in a lifetime. Use them. You chose them for a reason.

If anyone attempts to impose the feeling of wrongdoing or guilt on you, acknowledge their present fear as they are reflecting an aspect of you that needs to be acknowledged, addressed, and dismissed.

Then, you can proceed with remembering and developing your gifts, and doing the work you have planned for yourself in this lifetime.

Energy Transfer

Energy transfers and will take up residence in your body if you allow it to. Be mindful of those who dump their problems and leave. Be mindful of those who want to have random intimacy and leave. Be mindful of your energy when a person is around you.

Some people will come to you to take your energy. They will leave feeling good, while you are left feeling drained. Put up an impenetrable protective shield around you using visualization.

Be

To "Be" is Source in a space of awareness. Be contains all things and nothing. It is the space before creation as you know it. Be is the absence of light, where all things and possibilities exist.

Spiritual Sight

Spirit sees in all directions and does not limit itself to physical eyes. Turn out the lights and notice your senses heighten. You are seeing without the physical eyes. You are sensing, by feeling. Feeling, being connected to, or being aware of energy is the first communication. What do you feel?

Be more aware by practicing not relying on what you see in the light or with your physical eyes. Pay more attention to what you feel.

Distractions

This reality is fear-based to maintain control and give you, the protagonist, something to overcome. Distractions are necessary to keep you in a state of fear. Distractions keep you focused on survival and not knowing your power as a spirit being.

To know thyself is to know that you are first energy, second spirit, and then man. The body is a vessel of identification in this reality because as humans you are distant from your true self. The spirit animates the body. Learn about energy to know your power.

Everything is You

Everything you can see is you. Ultimately you are one being that has split to have many reflections to see herself and know, without doubt, that she exists. You are Source.

The same way a human body is a source of energy, with cells that have a life, identity, and purpose, you are a cell in this celestial body, Source.

When you speak ill of someone, you are speaking ill of yourself.

When you harm someone, you are harming yourself.

When you disrespect someone, you are disrespecting yourself.

Earth

Earth is the planet where the incarnated experience what Source experienced when she was in a state of Be, I, and then Knowing.

You experience "Be" when there is darkness. This is where Source questioned her existence.

You experience "I", which is identity, when the sun rises, and you can see color and all things in creation. This is the result of the Big Bang.

You experience the "Knowing," as you identify all the things that you are.

Cherish this experience. Look at this world with the wonder and curiosity of a child. Find the beauty in all things because they are you.

Reflections

Everyone is a reflection of you. They agreed to be a part of your story, appear at a certain time, and reflect a part of you that is ready to heal.

The very thing that irritates you about a person is within you. It is in your root experiences. It may take time to see yourself but with diligence, you will.

Going forward, approach your relationships with the question, "Friend, what are you here to teach me about myself?"

Focus & Manifestation

The universe/creation does not hear "no" or "do not." It pays attention to where you have focused your energy. Where you focus determines what you will manifest.

Emotions amplify energy. When the emotions fear and anger or gratitude and love are active, they aid in quick manifestation.

Owning Your Story

When you choose to own your story in this reality, you immediately take back your power. You are no longer a victim of circumstance.

Owning your story is acknowledging that you decided which lessons to learn and the roles people would play.

You cannot pick and choose which parts to own and when to be a victim. It is all or nothing. Either you are in control and accept your power or you are a pawn and being controlled.

Emotions Are Master Teachers

Emotions are spirit beings, energy, and master teachers. When you vibrate on their frequency, they arrive to make you aware that there is a lesson available or that you are ready to heal an aspect of yourself.

You can commune with emotions to understand their purpose in your life. Call them forth and ask questions. If you listen, you will get answers which will help you to heal more quickly.

Embrace emotions. They are companions of this reality.

Triggers

Triggers are uncomfortable feelings related to past experiences that signal you are ready to heal the original and related, subsequent experiences or patterns of behavior.

Triggers are not meant to be ignored. There is no need to get angry with anyone because they did not *make you* feel that emotion. It was you, signaling yourself that it is time to heal.

Dissect triggers by asking yourself, "When did I first feel this way?" The answer is in the root; your childhood experiences. See the pattern of behavior and how it impacted your life. Make the necessary changes to stop the pattern.

Truth

Your truth is your truth. There are different versions of the truth as there are perspectives. Do not waste time being angry about a different version of the truth. It is another perspective that you have no control over.

When you arrive at universal truths, they are undeniable. For example, water is wet.

Release Emotions

Emotions are meant to be experienced and released. If you are not in a state of peace, that emotion will stay there to remind you that there is something in your life that needs to be addressed.

Some will pack down the emotions, resulting in energetic imbalances in the body, thus activating the DNA and unlocking various propensities to illnesses.

Look at the patterns in your family concerning vices, illnesses, and experiences to learn what you have the potential to activate in your DNA when not addressing what needs to be healed within you.

Forgiveness

Forgiveness is unnecessary. You wrote the story. Everyone is playing a role in your story. There is no one to blame. No guilt or shame is needed if you take ownership of your existence. Everyone is doing what you asked them to do, regardless of who it is.

Empty Words

Some words and emotions cause you to act, like anger. Other words place you in limbo, like "hope" or "try." Some words place you in a space of inaction, like "doubt."

Look at the state of melanated people who lean on hope. Hope is waiting for someone else to take action. Instead of hoping, will it. Instead of trying, do!

Worry

Worry is misdirected focus. Worry is stagnant and only projects fear related to the feeling of not being in control.

Redirect your focus to the present moment, which is what you can control. Give gratitude for what you do have. Speak positivity into existence. Love changes things.

Doubt

Doubt fucks things up! Doubt is uncertainty. The moment you allow doubt to creep in, it changes the energy of whatever you may be manifesting. Instead of the energy being certain of what it is meant to bring into fruition, it is confused.

If you allow doubt in, immediately correct it with gratitude for what is coming.

Moments

Moments don't have a predefined measurement. They are as fleeting as a microsecond and as long as an experience.

We have moments within moments that are created by what we focus on.

Energetic Signatures

Each experience you have, when you heal, and what you change, changes the energetic signature of your earth family's DNA, plus your essence or higher self.

Choose the impact you desire to make. It will impact future generations.

Shhhh!

Be quiet about what you are working on because energy transfers. There is a saying, "The master never speaks of his work until it is complete." He knows that energy can be impacted by other energy.

Share your goals or desires with only those who you know for sure will lift and support you. All others with opposing energy will attach and impact your goals. When this occurs, most will either have difficulty with, or drop their dreams altogether.

As Above, So Below

This reality mirrors creation. As above, so below.

For example, the internet mirrors the overall consciousness, where all information is accessible.

Healing

Healing is delving into the painful experiences to understand why you chose them, the various levels and layers, to release energy, beliefs, and emotions that no longer serve you.

Create a void by releasing old energy. Fill it with love.

Kindness

Kindness is an energy born from love. Kind gestures are from the heart. They are done without expectation. They are acts of love.

All things should be done from the heart. Actions should be kind. This is a confirmation that you are not acting from fear-based emotions. This includes compromising self by being nice because of fear of not being acknowledged, loved, or accepted.

The Ego

The ego is a split or aspect of you that has emotional memory. It responds or protects based on what you have experienced and felt emotionally.

The ego keeps you in a safe space; what is known to be true and correct at that time. The ego knows what you can currently endure, until it is recalibrated by the changes you make in your life.

When you have good or beneficial experiences that are the opposite of fear, the ego releases the need to protect you from the past hurt. This stops the negative chatter which is the attempt to stop you from experiencing the unknown; something that you are not sure will not hurt you.

Limitations

Limitations are created from fear and the need to control. Part of your journey is to exceed assumed or self-imposed limitations. Break free from limitations by doing something you have been afraid to do.

Layers of Healing

You heal on four layers, spiritual, mental, physical, and emotional. As you heal one layer, another is exposed. You revisit past experiences to deepen your understanding of self.

Your Journey

You chose your experiences, lessons, family, abusers, allies, and friends before you arrived here. Every role you have assigned is filled by your spirit friend who agreed to be what you needed them to be, for you to experience the lessons you desired.

Fear and Love Manifests

Fear is equal to love when manifesting. Whatever you focus on, you give power to.

Your focus activates the necessary energy and assigns the task for creation to fulfill. The longer you focus on it, regardless if it is through love or fear, worry or happiness, you strengthen the power of the assigned energy to bring forth that thing.

Belief vs Knowing

Belief is giving power to something outside yourself. Knowing is within and directly connected to the collective consciousness.

Raising Consciousness

Every moment you choose to put love first, in words, thoughts and action, you are raising the consciousness and shifting this reality.

Green

Green is the color of love. If you ever feel unloved, go outside. You are surrounded by love. Green is the energy that sustains your life in this reality.

Illness

Illnesses are the manifestations of energetic imbalances. When pain or discomfort appears, it is the body signaling you that it is ready to heal. When it gets to the point of illness, you have let it go too far. The body is telling you that it needs immediate attention. It is time to do the work to heal on the emotional, mental, spiritual, and physical layers.

If you only address the physical symptoms and not the emotional, spiritual, and mental, the likelihood of the illness returning is high.

Discomfort

Discomfort is a signal that you are needing attention from yourself. It is time to accept and surrender to the very thing you have been avoiding. It is time to do the work to heal.

There is power in discomfort. There is a lesson for you. Get it.

Love

Love does not hurt. Expectations generate fear-based emotions resulting in pain.

Love is open arms. It does not hold onto anything or anyone. Love honors flow and change. It allows people and things to come and go, knowing that what is present will stay as long as it, or they are supposed to.

Masculine Dominance

This reality is currently dominated by masculine needs, definitions, and ego.

Masculine is mental and physical; logic and action.

Masculine has been taught that if they feel emotions, cry, or acknowledge the feminine aspects of self, they are weak.

Connecting with the feminine, which is spiritual and emotional, would develop compassion for the feminine and men would deepen their understanding as to why this reality is imbalanced. They would also balance themselves.

Feminine Imbalance

Feminine has gravitated toward the masculine aspects to function in this reality. To balance, the feminine must get in tune with femininity. They need to release the definition and ideas of feminine created by the masculine. Feminine must define feminine for herself.

Feminine & Masculine Balance

When two things are balanced, one is not heavier or greater than the other. Though they may be different, they have equal power.

To balance the feminine and masculine relationship, the feminine must remember who she is and the masculine must remember that feminine is equal.

When both stand in their true essence, there is respect and honor for the duality and what it represents as a balance to the opposite energy. To understand one, you must understand the other.

Soul Ties

Most of the beings that experience this life with you are familiar spirits that you have journeyed with in other lifetimes.

Your other lifetimes together and familiarity as kindreds, creates soul ties, or friendships from shared experiences. These are the beings that you feel like you have known forever.

Twin Flames

Twin flames are the emblazoned reflections that if honored, will allow you to deeply see yourself, without sugarcoating.

Twin flame relationships are available for deep shadow work. Deep attraction is necessary to keep the connection for those involved to have a reason to be present, especially when the intensity of the relationship can make one want to run away.

Look beyond what you think you want and see yourself; the nervous, emotional, and mental imbalances related to the love you feel and do the work to correct them. When you do so, the love will balance itself and you will attract a love that mirrors the love you have for yourself.

Reflections of Love

Everyone in your life reflects your current level of self-love. It is demonstrated in how you relate to one another.

To manifest a greater love, give the love that you wish to receive to yourself.

Power of Observation

The ability to step back mentally, spiritually, and emotionally from a situation allows you to view it without connection to the events and outcome. Doing this allows you to see multiple perspectives and make decisions for the greatest good of all involved.

The power of observation is one of the best tools for self-work. Observe your habits, actions, reactions, and complacency. See yourself.

Authority

Release everything that places authority or belief in man over you. Listen to those who promote a deeper understanding of self, your power as an individual, and your power as an aspect of One.

Fear and Desire

Everything you desire is on the other side of fear. Fear likes to creep in through your back. It is sneaky and does not want to be noticed until it is too late. By then you are in its grasp, wondering how to get out. Fear poses as emotions such as anger, depression, anxiety, and more.

You have power over emotions. Simply call out fear by acknowledging the energy, stating what you fear, why you fear it, and take action to change. You can also take a moment and ask fear, itself, what it is there to teach you.

Fear is greedy and gluttonous. It will stay and suck on your energy as long as you allow it. It is common in this existence and cocky about how it will thrive.

Nine Year Life Cycles

You have nine-year life cycles. The energy of each year builds on the last to manifest whatever you have focused on in the eighth year. Plan your cycles from the beginning knowing that you are building. Odd number years are for action. Even number years are for grounding.

Calculate your current personal year by adding your birth month, birthday, and current year. Continue adding and reducing until you get to a number between 1-9.

Example: May 7, 1970 = 5+7+1+9+7+0 = 29 2+9=11 1+1=2
1: Newness/New beginnings
2: Partnering/Patience/Duality
3: Networking/Happiness
4: Foundation/Grounding
5: Change/Physical form
6: Creativity/Responsibility
7: Introspection/Spirituality
8: Reap/ Success
9: Endings/Release

No One Owes You

No one owes you and you owe no one. Anything you do should be from love and kindness, not from indebtedness.

You have agreements with your parents, friends, and others to show up in your life exactly as they have, for you to learn about yourself. You are sharing experiences in their lives as agreed for them to learn about themselves.

No one owes anyone because of what emotions were felt during an experience. Each experience is an opportunity for you to learn and heal.

Releasing Victimhood

Victimhood is a cushion for some, who want to garner empathy or sympathy from another. Speaking and living in that space is a cry for love. That person wants to be heard, understood, and protected.

You release victimhood when you own your life, knowing you wrote your story. Any person that has harmed you, did so, at your request, for you to learn about and heal from painful experiences. It is a lesson for you to learn to love yourself in spite of what happened and know that you are worthy of love. You are love.

Answers From Your Heart

You have all the answers within. Your heart (chakra) is the largest brain in the body. When you want to know your truth, put your hand on your heart and focus on it. Ask your question out loud, while maintaining focus on your heart. This is necessary for you to not focus on the mind and attempt to sort it out with logic. Speak the answer immediately.

If you catch yourself thinking, you must redirect your focus to your heart so the answer is pure and not one of ego.

Divination Tools

Divination tools are a point of focus for you to tune into the knowing.

There are many divination tools crafted to provide insight and glimpses of the past and future. These tools are in addition to your natural intuitive abilities.

Fear of divination tools was created for control. This fear teaches you to fear your power. Embrace divination tools and your ability to see, predict, and know possibilities.

Your Voice

Every reality has laws as to what is accessible, what can happen, and what can be used. In this reality, your voice is one of the most powerful vehicles of change that you have access to.

Sound is transformational. Your voice is sound. It can immediately impact energy through vibration and frequency.

Be mindful of the intent and energy of your words. Be mindful of what you listen to. Words and the force within your voice can either lift or destroy. It is your choice to create life or create death.

Fight or Ease

To call something a fight or to say you have been fighting all your life, means you have been calling in an energy that is in opposition to what you truly want to happen.

You called in difficulty instead of ease. You called in the need to overcome. Erase fight from your vocabulary in reference to anything you desire to accomplish. Instead claim that all things you desire easily flow to you.

Health

The way to truly heal is to address the energetic imbalances which include stored and unexpressed emotions. The imbalances are unresolved traumas, hurts, and pains that impact certain areas of the body.

Address them by expressing, accepting, and releasing.

That Is Not Love

If a person is attacking you or being unloving in their approach to you, you do not have to stay for, or tolerate that experience. Consider reminding them that, "that is not love," and remove yourself from the situation.

You teach people how to treat you by what you tolerate. Do not confuse this with consistently removing yourself from a repetitive relationship type. If it is repetitive, there is a lesson there for you and until you see the reflection and get the lesson, you will continue to attract the same.

A person does not have to be physically present for you to review your actions in a relationship and make the changes within yourself to stop a cycle.

You have fail-safes in your story. If you run from the lesson, you wrote in additional people to appear to reflect what needs to be healed.

To Flow

To flow is to be free of ideas, conditions, and/or concepts of who or where you should be, and/or what you should be doing.

Flowing requires you to release control, worry, doubt, and fear. Flowing invites you to live in the knowing that you are always in the right place and time, at all times.

Flowing releases questioning whether you are going in the right direction because you know that wherever you are headed is correct for you. There is an experience awaiting you.

Whatever is for you is for you. There is no need to question or worry. Mind your focus and it will mind you.

Failure is Not an Option

Words are used to control people and their emotions. The controlling emotions are those that are fear-based and failure is one of those words.

Claiming failure erases effort and what you have accomplished. Embracing failure is a form of conditioning to make you feel "less than" or "insufficient."

This reality is layered and built on experiences that you are meant to have and grow from. What if, instead of calling yourself a failure, you instead said, "I have had an experience?"

By changing your perspective, you change the energy. By changing the energy, you take back your power. Never allow yourself or anyone else to call you a failure.

Stress

Stress depletes the body of necessary nutrients for cells to function properly which results in imbalances and disease.

Many people are likely living in a high-functioning stressful environment. They are required to do, be and act to survive, no matter the circumstance.

Energy is currency. Examine how you spend your energy. Are you giving away your energy to people and situations, to be liked, loved, or thought of as being a good person?

When people live in harmony, stress is reduced. It is up to you to first create harmony in your life by eliminating as much stress as possible.

Letting Go

When you hold on to people, energy, and things, you are not allowing the flow of new energy into your life. Holding on when you know you should release creates tension. The energy wants to move because it has served its purpose in your life.

Letting go creates a void that creation will acknowledge and rush in to fill with new opportunities and experiences.

Letting go without worry or concern, is you knowing that you wrote a story where you are always taken care of. Whatever you need or desire will appear, in and on time.

Blessings

It has become easy for people to believe that everything they pray for is being answered by a god, outside of themselves. It is easier for them to let go of their concern or worry because they believe that a being is going to answer their prayers.

What if when you pray you are practicing true manifestation? Manifesting requires knowing that all things in creation already exist. When you set the energy free it will work and return to you what you are seeking.

You are God, the Creator, Source, and Universe. Whatever you focus on will manifest. You are praying to and blessing yourself. You are your blessing.

Black. Dark. The Absence of Light.

In this reality, you have been conditioned to believe that the hue, black, is bad no matter if it is a skin tone, an idea of religion, thought, or action.

Melanated people were conditioned to believe that having melanin is bad, distasteful, or something that needs to be discarded, when it is a complement to nature and existence.

In religions such as Vodun, the practices have been called dark or black magic by those in power to scare the curious people away from it.

Everything in creation exists in darkness. You were born of darkness. Darkness or black is the reflection of the beginning of all things. Instead of running from black or dark, run to it. You are called hu(e)man for a reason.

Your Focus is Currency

Each day, media platforms are vying for your attention. Television, social media, and any platform that requires your attention for the owner to make money are making money from your focus; your energy. They are making money from you but what are you getting in return?

Learn to use these outlets to benefit you. Invest in yourself. Redirect your focus to what will create a more fulfilled and stress-free life.

Rejection

Rejection is looked at as a bad thing because of the emotions and thoughts that rise to the surface. Those emotions and thoughts are signals that a part of you is ready to heal. It is time for you to see yourself, behavior, and actions that create the situations you find yourself in.

Rejection is a signal that something is not right for you or it is time for an experience to end. Instead of denying or questioning the rejection, embrace it. You have the opportunity to create a void to be filled with a new experience.

Rejection points you in the right direction!

Boundaries

To set a boundary is to enforce a demarcation of what you will and will not allow in your life. The lack of boundaries in your life is permitting people to do what they will without thought as to how it is impacting you.

You are teaching people how to treat you by what you accept in your life.

Set boundaries to take back your power, increase respect, and love in your life.

Tears, Laughter, and Screaming

You always have a supply of healing tools available within you. Tears, laughter, and screaming are all expressions to help you release, shift energy, cleanse and heal. Do not hold back. Your healing is in your hands.

The Root

The Root is the foundation of beliefs, fears, and ideas of what is right or wrong based on your childhood experiences. Your foundation sets up your lessons and what you will work to heal from in your lifetime.

ALL healing begins in the root. This is the place where all your responses come from and where you will be triggered to heal.

Identity

You give power to and become what you answer to. Be mindful of what you allow people to call you. When you continuously answer to a new alias or epithet, you are splitting yourself into another identity.

Emotions + Words

You have the power to change your perspective and immediately change the vibration of your story with words and emotions. Words are spoken but it is the emotion behind the words that direct the energy.

Change your emotions and words when speaking about your situation.

Eliminate Dependency

Practice eliminating the dependency on any being's assistance with your journey. Guides will show up as agreed but you are the key to understanding yourself.

Look within to access your power. You can tap into energy whenever you are ready. If you don't know the frequency or energetic address of the energy you'd like to access, call it to you. Ask yourself, Source, for direction.

By eliminating dependency, you allow yourself to discover your power and possibilities.

Spirit Relationships

Treat spirit beings as equals to you. Respect their abilities as you would desire the same respect for your abilities.

Though the physical body of a person has died, the spirit is still accessible. You can reach out to beings such as Albert Einstein, Ludwig Beethoven, Michael Jackson, Zora Neale Hurston, or Malcolm X to converse, get help, and enhance your creativity, knowledge, or enlightenment.

Call them forth. Give an offering. Make a request and listen.

Your Frequency Shift

Sudden growth and development are necessary for you to arrive at a certain frequency for you to continue your mission.

It may be uncomfortable. You wrote your journey to include rising to a higher vibration regardless of where you are in your story if you haven't already done so at your own will.

You will always be able to handle what you have chosen. Perspective is the key. Have you chosen this for yourself or is this happening to you? Your answer dictates your outcome. Either you will be a victim or the conductor.

Unexpected Power

Power is in the eye of the beholder. You can be powerful in silence or speech, action or inaction, and love or anger. There are many variances in power. It is all in how you use the energy and what is appropriate for that moment.

Teach yourself to not do the expected. At that moment, you will understand how to use your power.

5D

The massive deaths that occurred due to the "pandemic" were necessary as the bodies could not sustain the energy shift. They chose to leave the earthly experience to make room for the new masters who will continue to help raise the love vibration.

To sustain the energy of 5D, one must operate in pure love.

5D increases the perspectives of this existence, providing the ability to travel and move in and out of dimensions. 5D decreases the need for the physical form as many will return to their original knowledge of creation and focus on energy.

The awareness of your connection to all things is deepened. Compassion is increased with the understanding that what you do to someone you are doing to yourself.

Touch Soil

Touch soil often. Soil contains the ingredients and DNA of all that has been created on the planet Earth.

Soil can amplify and heal your body by providing vital energetic connections to your system. Therefore it is important to walk barefoot.

The elements, earth, air, water, and fire, directly impact your physical healing abilities.

Gather and Share Knowledge

Explore and share knowledge. People are sharing spiritual knowledge on social media programs that you already have access to.

Since many of you deny your ability to connect to Source and receive downloads, you have to be met where you are and fed the spiritual information you need through media.

Temper your spiritual connection by testing it daily with meditation. Still your focus. Ask a question. Listen for the answer.

Not all meditation requires you to be physically still. You can walk, wash dishes, or be driving and get downloads. Meditation is a shift in focus that grants access to a stream of information.

All That Is and Nothing

Go to the space of BE (beginning) by closing your eyes and focusing on the darkness. The beginning of all things is in darkness. This is the space of all that is and nothing.

BE appears as nothingness because you do not see anything but darkness. Darkness may be equated to nothingness because you have not tapped into a physical form within the darkness.

You must know the energetic address to tap into realities, dimensions, or spirit beings. When you tune in to a frequency by matching the vibration, you discover that everything exists in darkness.

A particular frequency houses energy or energies that you can connect to. The earthly experience has a frequency. You have a frequency. Everything and nothing that exists in the absence of light has a frequency that is the equivalent of an energetic signature.

Sight and Sound

Sight and sound can be deceptive at times. They are both used to calibrate you to lower frequencies for control.

Pay attention to the news that you receive on a spiritually powerful day. Those in control will manipulate you through what you see and hear so you are not in a highly energetic space to use the available energy.

Fun software has been designed to keep you distracted and engaged to track where you are and what you currently look like.

You currently have access to software that allows you to change your face to another's face. At a moment's notice, your image can be used for whatever purpose.

Everything is not what it seems. Doubt everything you are being fed by your government or whoever is in power until it resonates with you.

Happiness is a Distraction

Happiness is a distraction to keep you controlled. You are conditioned to measure your reality against happiness which is fleeting. Accepting that happiness is an emotion like other emotions, and is not necessarily sustained over a long period, relieves you from attempting to attain a continuous state of being.

There is power in peace. Peace is a foundation and building block of all things in balance. Peace is attainable and is a better focal point along with stress reduction.

Breaking Down

Many of you feel that it is a weakness to break down, cry, or not be aligned with what is happening in your life.

To experience a release of energy is not a weakness. It is you signaling that it is time for a big change or transformation as you have outgrown the current programming.

Harmony With Nature

Continue to spend time in harmonious spaces in this existence. Something as simple as gardening grants you more autonomy and peace, with the knowledge that you are not dependent on manufacturers, farmers, or shippers to feed you.

Fright

Fright is necessary to shake and shape your awareness. You've written moments into your story to remind you to stay alert and aware of your surroundings.

Ghosts

Every spirit or ghost that inhabits your dwelling is not meant to be gotten rid of. You have agreements with them as well. Ask their purpose before kicking them out. Some are ancestors or angels. Some are protectors.

Speak to Release

Communicate. Don't hold anything in. To change the energy you must move it. Speaking is one of the quickest ways to move stagnant and potentially harmful energy from your body.

You do not have to be in the presence of anyone to speak what you feel. The moment you think of or speak someone's name, their energy is present.

Languages Will Eventually Be Defunct

When the collective returns to the first communication which is feeling energy, communication with spoken words will not be necessary.

Pay attention to what you feel when communicating. People can be deceptive in their communication with language. A person can say they are happy but their energy does not exude happiness.

What you feel will lead you to the facts when not overshadowed by your emotions and ego.

The Only Goal

Love is the only goal. Raising the earthly consciousness requires you to do one thing. Love. Remember that you are love and exude it first to yourself and then to all relations.

About Kijana

Kijana is a spiritual guide, psychic channel, master teacher, public speaker, and medicine woman. She began her spiritual journey as a child, never speaking of her gifts as she had assumed that everyone had the same experiences. Kijana has been communing with the spirit world, consciously, since she was a teenager.

In 2010, she left the corporate world and became a professional development coach, facilitating close to 100 proprietary workshops for government agencies, nonprofit and spiritual organizations.

In 2013, her life began to change as she was redirected to delve deeper into spirituality and hone her skills. She took time to focus on her healing to be a better guide to others.

In 2016, Kijana decided to experience entheogens beginning with Ayahuasca. It was in her first Ayahuasca journey that she began channeling. A couple of months later, during her experience with psilocybin, the Council of 12 introduced themselves to her.

What had been a somewhat frightening experience has led her to be a conduit for the Council of 12's teachings and guidance for hundreds of people. She hosts a variety of events, retreats, and private sessions for those seeking healing.

She can be reached at www.kijanaunplugged.com.

www.ingramcontent.com/pod-product-compliance
Lightning Source LLC
Chambersburg PA
CBHW020943090426
42736CB00010B/1247